How Much Joy is in Your Journey?

A Creative Guide to Your Fearless Vision

Dr. Ja'net Bishop, Ed.D

How Much Joy Is In Your Journey?
A Creative Guide To Your Fearless Vision

Published by:

Have Joy, LLC

First edition copyright c 2016, Dr. Ja'net Bishop, Ed.D

Cover design by:

Michael Matulka
gobasik.com

Printed in the United States of America
ISBN-10: 0-692-60645-9
ISBN-13: 978-0-692-60645-2

I dedicate this book …

To my husband William, and our sons William II and
Matthew,
     …. for their love and support with every '*new*' idea I've
     conjured up over the years!

To my parents James and Carrie Smalls,
     …. for instilling in me that with '*faith*', all things are
     possible!

To my brothers Darryl and James,
     …. who always made me feel like I was the best sister
     that brothers could hope for! *I claim it*!

To my community of family and friends,
     …. who've encouraged me in so many ways with,
     "*You can do that*!"

Contents

Introduction

"The one trait that all successful, fulfilled people cultivate - be they great writers, teachers, entrepreneurs, artists, parents, politicians, or athletes —is a passion and enthusiasm for life. We all need a compelling vision for our lives: one so powerful that we are driven to do whatever it takes to achieve it."
-Anthony Robbins

Joy

[joi]

NOUN

1. The emotion of great delight or happiness caused by something exceptionally good or satisfying; keen pleasure; elation. Emotion evoked by well-being, success, or by the prospect of possessing what one desires.
2. A source or cause of keen pleasure or delight; something or someone greatly valued or appreciated.
3. The expression or display of glad feeling; festive
gaiety.

VERB (USED WITHOUT OBJECT)

6. To feel joy; be glad; rejoice.
(http://www.merriam-webster.com/dictionary/joy)

Life is meant to be lived abundantly! Many people in Western culture are striving for success. There are people who make a lot of money, but their relationships "stink". There are people who are highly spiritual, but they're broke all of the time. There are people who want the home, a great business and all of these outer things. However, having these outer things does not guarantee what we really want, which is happiness. We go for these outer things thinking that they're going to bring us the happiness, but it's backwards.

The way to live that abundant life is to go for the inner joy, the inner peace, and the inner vision first, and then all of the outer things appear. Everything you want is actually an "inside" job. The "outside" world is a world of effects. It's just the results of your thoughts. Life is meant to be abundant. Set your thoughts on happiness and joy!

You hold the key to more abundance in every area of your life than you can possibly imagine. You deserve every good thing that you want and the universe will give you every good thing that you want, but you have to summon it into your life. You have the key. The key is your thoughts and feelings that you will use to manifest your vision. What you probably don't realize is that you've been holding the key in your hands all of your life.

If you don't know where you're going, it's going to be hard to get there. You may have a general idea about which direction you want to travel in your personal life, but sometimes it's not easy. It can be difficult to determine what you want from your work life beyond the expected measures of achievement: a terrific salary, professional recognition and promotions. Have you considered which path to travel that will allow you to use your gifts and talents, enjoy the steps in the journey, and bring you satisfying success with joy?

Imagine living a life of purpose where you get to do what you want and you get to enjoy doing it. Imagine getting rid of the self-defeating chatter in your mind, those nagging voices that chip away at your self-esteem and prevents you from accomplishing your goals or dreams. Imagine developing the courage and confidence to maximize your own true potential and experience more joy in your personal and professional life because you have developed and explored a vision for your life.

Every successful life endeavor, business, or organization requires a vision which leads to a plan. Believe that no enterprise is more essential than the business of your own life. Having a clear vision of where you are and what you are pursuing is very important. If you have no vision, the moving toward the destination may cause you to find yourself going around and around in circles, and you wonder why you're feeling "stuck" and getting nowhere!

Like a business, you need a vision from which your mission and a strategic plan can be developed. This will help you to remain passionate and engaged in your work. If the idea of creating a strategic vision and plan for your life so that you can experience more fulfilling joy causes you to think, "I'd rather have my tooth pulled," believe that this can be a concise, enjoyable process that enables you to focus on what's really important. Creating a good vision for your life is crucial to being successful in life.

ABOUT THE CONTENTS

The premise of this book is to assist you in creating your vision; the road map for the path on which you will travel. I invite you to join me as we explore coaching as a way to empower yourself and improve your life, becoming more of who you are, sharing your best self with others, and creating deep and lasting change in serving others. Consider using this book as a guide in creating your vision to be more closely aligned in your personal and professional life.

This book will be particularly beneficial for the following audiences:

* *Entrepreneurs and employees,
* *Leaders and aspiring leaders,
* *Homemakers and empty nesters,
* *Career-Builders and those in transition,
* *Visionaries and those who make the vision come true,
* *Nurturers, Counselors, and Coaches,
* *Mentors and mentees,
* *Plus … the people who've decided that they want more.

THE APPROACH

As we prepare to travel together through this guidebook, let me share about my approach to this topic. I don't profess to be an expert on creating the perfect life vision because I'm the most successful person that I know. That would be pretty over-blown on my part! What I have found in my leadership and coaching experiences with adults, through counseling experiences with students over the years, as well as graduate degrees in the field of counseling and leadership - is that a person without vision will perish. So, here's my very practical approach that you'll find in this book:

Inspirational quotes. If you're like me, having bursts of insight to inspire working hard is energizing sometimes. If you haven't looked up from the laptop long enough, your vision can get cloudy. Quotes throughout this book serves as reminders that there's a purpose and reason for your dedication, discipline, and hard work.

Real-life stories of people with experiences that you may be able to relate to, who were able to clarify their vision, embraced their purpose, and found the joy that identified their true definition of personal success and created their path towards professional achievement.

Reflective insights that will enable you to identify your qualities, gifts, and natural strengths. You will tap into your own personal power.

Coaching questions to help you clarify your follow-up steps. As you strive towards more success, know that asking the right questions facilitates finding the right answers for the experience that you are trying to work through.

Resources that you may find helpful in further exploration along your journey.

This book will guide you through new insights to help you develop your strategy for your vision for your personal and professional life - to be more aligned with your values. It is an investment in your well-being. Through life experience and formal education, we may learn a great deal about the road we travel to success and joy. Some of what we learn may be right on the mark, and then some of what we've been exposed to surface as speed-bumps, or obstacles, that get in the way of our growth in areas that are important to us. These areas may be ever-evolving, and changing within the different seasons of life that we may be travelling through. Even though life may have twists and turns, and unexpected set-backs shakes us off the balance we thought we had, it's critical that you understand the main points of your own overall well-being.

You are about to take the first steps in your journey within a coaching framework, that is constructed to help you clarify your life's vision and lead to enhancing your well-being, and increasing your joy and productivity. You will begin thinking and moving forward in such a way that supports you accomplishing the vision that you have for your life.

As you take this journey with me, I will share various topics addressing why you need a vision, how to create your vision, identifying what you really want, constructing what your best life would look like, and some tips for having joy in your workplace. Yes, the "destination" is important, but let's embrace and enjoy the journey. Like taking a walk in the park, you know where it is you want to go from one point to another, but as you travel—you *feel* the experience and you'll notice things along the way that were previously overlooked while you were hastily running through life. You'll listen to nature and enjoy the view through this meditative experience. There's no race. Just you, your inner voice, and self-coaching for clarity.

> *"Take delight in the Lord*
> *and he will give you the desires of your heart."*
> *-Psalm 37:4*

Are you ready? Okay, let's get started!

Ja'net

CHAPTER 1

What's Special About Coaching?

"We have enough people who tell it like it is—
Now we could use a few who tell it like it can be."
-Robert Orben

Steps Toward Joy

1. Identify what you love doing and what drains your energy.
2. Become clear about your values.

****

<u>My Story</u>

Coaching embraced me in a very unique way; not straightforward, but through a winding path at a crossroads. I'm a wife, mother, daughter, and sister. I'm a friend. I'm a veteran Army officer who was also a military wife, which was a very interesting combination! As a civilian, I've worked in non-profit organizations on behalf of at-risk youth, and in the K-12 traditional and non-traditional school settings as a School Counselor, a School Principal, and as an Adjunct Professor in higher education.

I've always felt it was my purpose in life to help people be the best that they can be. It was January 2014 when I first read about coaching, and thought "that's me!" It was a new approach to help others discover how to live their lives fully with purpose and in accord with their personal strengths. I believe in the power of coaching. I believe its strategies can transform lives as clients work towards clarifying their life vision and manifesting more joy in their lives. As a believer, I acquired a coach, and my thoughts have soared as I was propelled into action!

Through the coaching training at the Center for Applied Positive Psychology (CaPP) Institute, (founded by well-known life coach and author) Valorie Burton, I became certified as a Personal and Executive Coach. What an amazing and empowering experience it has been! I've led workshops and groups for over 20+years, and I believe that I am a better spouse, parent, friend, and educator—having had the coaching experience. I was eager to learn more about coaching and interested in finding ways to be of service to others.

The need for us all to be well-prepared leaders in our personal and professional lives is great today. This book is one effort to help meet that demand. It evolves from the realization that we are facing huge challenges from many directions. In the midst of living your life, you have varied duties and you fulfill multiple roles – both new ones and traditional ones – and you may be trying to do all of them well. I believe in seizing joy and happiness along the way of experiencing life. As you are inspired to create a vision for this next path in your life, consider the following five major life areas which are interconnected in making our lives whole, and how joy and happiness might be manifested through the experience:

1. Spiritual
2. Emotional/Physical
3. Work
4. Relationships
5. Leisure/Recreational

*"It's always worthwhile
to make others aware of their worth."*
-Malcolm Forbes

Coaching Defined

*Coaching is not targeted at psychological illnesses. It is unlike therapy in that it does not focus on examining the past or diagnosing mental dysfunctions. Instead, coaching focuses on effecting change in a client's current and future behavior. It is a practice focused on helping clients determine and achieve personal and professional goals.

*Coaching is the collaborative and intentional process that guides you towards the actions that best reflect your values, vision, and mission. Through coaching questions, reflection, and *"aha"* moments followed by action - the coaching experience helps you to explore and expand your available options. This experience facilitates accountability that supports your forward movement and ultimately accelerates your progress.

*Coaching is based on your strengths. It emphasizes that people are *whole, complete, and resourceful* as they are. The coach's role is to help bring an individual's strengths to the foreground and move the individual to engage in the right actions to improve their personal and/or work lives. The coach is at once: teacher, guide, cheerleader, visionary, keeper of the vision, and process agent; facilitating meaningful linkages between inner and outer work in the lives of clients. To be "whole" refers to the whole self, for which career, family and friends, health, spirituality, finances, and physical environment matter.

*Coaching often begins with identifying core values, sense of purpose, and vision of the client in collaboration with the coach. A client works from the inside out, from examining their own passions, goals, and abilities to clarifying a more fulfilling life or work path. The coach facilitates the journey by asking probing questions, providing empathy, confronting, and sometimes training. As well, the coach's job is to extract from the client a vision and a plan for taking action toward realizing a new future. Similar to a sports coach, the coach works primarily in the present and is focused on doing what needs to be done to get to where they want to go. As coach, we want the client to experience wins and achievements. Wins - even small ones - can transform the client's outlook, as well as produce concrete results in major, lasting, and generalizable ways.

In my own coaching practice, improving professional

and personal satisfaction is the primary issue for which clients seek services. These clients vary from those who are suffering job displacement, are looking to escape the stresses of corporate America, or are under-earning and want to improve their careers. Coaching those in the non-profit sector and human service fields, has helped some to become energized and creative in addressing some of the frustrating social issues that exist in our communities. Non-profit leaders are often torn between enormous demands of providing for their organizations, and their personal lives. Coaching is an obvious choice to help those leaders to successfully prioritize and attempt to balance demands on their time, personal and organizational resources, and become more effective at delegating and focusing on what is most important.

"Twenty years from now, you will be more disappointed by the things that you didn't do than by the ones you did do. So throw off the bowlines. Sail away from the safe harbor. Catch the trade winds in your sails. Explore. Dream. Discover."
-Mark Twain

Coaching and You

Another way to look at coaching is to consider why people seek it. The vast majority of individuals who seek coaching are looking for career, business, or some form of self-development. They may want to pursue their life's dream; which might include changing jobs, advancing in their current company, starting a business, dealing with a difficult life event - or perhaps writing a book, or starting a non-profit. Coaching is simply a set of skills to help people do better and be better.

Coaching is a strategy used to inspire, motivate, and evoke positive change in the lives of others. As a coach, I inspire clients to take action and facilitate their strategy towards success in their chosen endeavor. Coaching is a tool used to solve a problem or to reach a goal.

Would you like to become *"un-stuck"* in your health, reduce stress, and create more balance in your life? Perhaps you desire a stronger sense of community and desire embracing a larger experience. Would you like to change something in particular about your life? You are not by yourself. Increasingly, people just like you and I, have been exhausted by the fast pace of our environment and want to explore lives of a higher quality. Lives where there's more time for yourself and your relationships, and more focus to envision a richer life with improved spiritual, emotional, and physical well-being.

Whether you're an educator, a business owner, a college graduate, a homemaker, a single parent trying to raise a family, or a hard-working employee, you may have experienced stress and burn out. You're wrestling with a sense of direction to align the values of your personal and professional life so that you can experience more joy in this journey of life, and not simply travel with your focus towards your destination. You know, it is difficult at times waiting to get that next job, or that contract, or for your spouse to say, "it's your turn to pursue your dreams", or until your children grow up and leave home, or until you get that promotion that you've been working hard to be noticed for. Perhaps it's time to take a step back, look at your priorities, and make a decision about getting clear on your values and what type of future you would like to begin to create. Where do you turn when you are searching for clarity to your life's vision? Now is as good a time as any to start!

Clarity Exercise

Before travelling a new path or exploring a new set of skills, it is helpful to "clear" old thoughts, beliefs, and feelings that might serve as obstacles to achieve what you want. Creating a vision and setting goals is difficult to accomplish if there are previous conflicts that undermine your belief system. Some of the techniques for achieving clarity includes bodywork: psychotherapy, yoga, Tai Chi, or meditation. You may find it helpful to have a journal or notebook to capture your thoughts. Writing in this book may be another way for you to "seize the moment" in taking action in your own progress. Go For It!

A set of questions listed in the Professional and Personal Inventory that follows, will help you gain clarity with your thoughts.

Complete the following questionnaire:

Self-Exploration:

Professional and Personal Inventory

-What are your current goals? Your long-term goals?

-What is your most significant obstacle to attaining your goals (a boss, money, mate, family, distractions, bad habits, fatigue, etc.)?

-What actions have you taken to accomplish your goals?

-What actions worked well? What actions did not work well?

-What accomplished goals are you most proud of?

-If you did not have to worry about money or other people's opinion of you, what would you be doing with your life?

-Who or what would you prefer to eliminate from your life?

-What is one thing you would want to do that would make the most profound difference in your life? Why?

(Note: Downloadable blank form on www.HaveJoyLLC.com)

"Success is not the key to happiness.
Happiness is the key to success.
If you love what you are doing, you will be successful."
—Albert Schweitzer

List 5 Things You Love to Do:

1.

_____

2.

_____

3.

_____

4.

_____

5.

_____

(Note: Downloadable blank form on www.HaveJoyLLC.com)

Energy Drains

Energy drains are situations, events, and people that you tolerate in your life that rob you of your energy and impede you from enjoying life and being yourself to the highest degree. Energy drains can be like a tire with a nail in it. You keep "driving" along and "air"/ "energy drains" keeps seeping out the more you travel to your destinations. Energy drains can range from small chores such as doing grocery shopping, to more significant personal challenges, such as a person whose mate refuses to commit to their relationship.

Let's explore your energy drains, write down at least five (5) things you can think of that you would no longer want to tolerate in your life. If you continue exploring your thoughts, you probably can pinpoint many more energy drains at this time in your life. Funny how the list can seem to continue to grow as you start counting!

List 5 Energy Drains in Your *Professional* Life:	List 5 Energy Drains in Your *Personal* Life:
1.	1.
2.	2.
3.	3.
4.	4.
5.	5.

(Note: Downloadable blank form on www.HaveJoyLLC.com)

"We are what we repeatedly do.
Excellence, therefore, is not an act ... but a habit."
—Aristotle

Life is complex and multifaceted. To build capacity in life, we need to navigate around and push beyond our limits. We need ways to replenish our energy reserves. We need to be able to effectively balance the flow of energy that we release, as well as the energy required to rejuvenate ourselves to accomplish our goals. We cannot be at our best unless we pay attention to that which drains us, as well as that which energizes us to travel our true path and embrace the journey.

Clarifying Values — *"Walk the Walk & Talk the Talk"*

From this alphabetized list of 'Values' (on pages 19 through 22), choose 10 values (or add your own). Next, rank your 10 personal values according to their importance to you in the 'Importance' column. Finally, in the 'Behavior' column, rank order your same 10 values in terms of how you *actually* live. As you examine your values and behavior, notice whether or not you actually behave according the the values that you identify as important. Does this suggest any changes you might consider making?

(Note: Downloadable blank form on www.HaveJoyLLC.com)

Values	Importance	Behavior
Accomplishments(s)		
Achievement		
Adventure/Excitement		
Aesthetics/Beauty		
Athleticism		
Altruism		
Authenticity		
Autonomy		
Clarity		
Collaboration		
Commitment		

Value	Importance	Behavior
Community		
Compassion		
Connection/Bonding		
Creativity		
Decisiveness		
Ease		
Emotional Health		
Environment		
Family/Family First		
Financial Freedom/Wealth		
Fitness		
Freedom		
Fun		
Health/Well-being		
Honesty		
Humor		
Integrity		
Intimacy		
Joy		

Value	Importance	Behavior
Leadership		
Lifelong Learning		
Love		
Loyalty		
Making a Difference		
Mastery/Excellence		
Mediating differences		
Moving things forward		
Openness		
Orderliness/accuracy		
Partnership		
Philanthropy		
Power		
Privacy/Solitude		
Recognition/Acknowledgement		
Religion		
Risk taking		
Romance		
Security		

Value	Importance	Behavior
Self-expression		
Sensuality		
Service/contribute (as in "servant leader)		
Spirituality		
Success		
Trust		
Vitality		
Wisdom		
Other:_____ _____ _____ _____		

(Note: Downloadable blank form on www.HaveJoyLLC.com)

"… the fruit of the spirit is Joy"
-Galatians 5:22

Reflection:

Summarizing Clarifying Your Values

Our values impact and may direct our quality of life.

-What do you value (see the previous Clarifying Value activity on pages 22 - 25)?

-Is the quality of your work and personal life compatible with your values?

- Does this suggest any changes you might consider making so that your professional and personal behaviors are more aligned with your values, enabling more joy to be present in your life?

(Note: Downloadable blank form on   www.HaveJoyLLC.com)

Holistic (Whole) Life

Let's begin to take a closer look at the life that you're living. One way to live beyond having a life that centers around work, is to become aware of the areas that may be "falling through the cracks". Life consists of many dimensions, and neither one can be considered more important than the other. However, there may be times when you find yourself focusing more in one area than another. As I experience more in life, it becomes clearer to me that having *balance* is a myth. We should aspire towards having a *flow* through different areas of our lives. Some areas may get 20% of our time one week and at other times, 80%, or vice versa. What you must know is that you have permission to expand your vision and your life beyond work to other areas—your spiritual life, emotional/physical life, work life, relationships with others, and leisure. By spending some time in each of these areas, you'll become increasingly aware of what's missing—or, needed in your life.

Where might your life be out of *flow*? What gets most of your attention and time? What are the areas that you have put on hold or have been neglecting? You, like most people, may wish that you had more time to spend with loved ones, devote to your health and fitness, or to have fun.

You can create your life in a way that you are able to spend time more evenly distributed among each of these areas. With an honest assessment of what gets your attention and the willingness to take action, you can bring your life into a more systematic ebb and flow.

Awareness comes first; then you must take the actions needed to make a change.

Spiritual

Well-being in your spiritual life may mean different things to different people. For some, developing a spiritual life works within a religious context; going to a specific house of worship, or perhaps studying religious texts. For many, a sense of peace and centeredness that evolves from spending time in meditation or nature, or studying different spiritual practices is what being connected to the spiritual is all about. One usually needs to feel connected to the divine in some way. Whatever you choose, you'll be honoring your spiritual well-being and creating an inner security that will expose you to experiencing that which connects all of us. *What condition is your spiritual life? In what way is it different than in your younger years? What does "spiritual well-being" mean to you?* Write about it in your journal.

Emotional/Physical

Emotions have a major impact on our physical health. Caring for your emotional health may mean making time for respite, reflection, and solitude—or having a good laugh with others. Embracing what makes you feel good and building that into your daily schedule will raise your spirits, keep your attitude upbeat, and protect your general health. *Think about a time when you felt relaxed and peaceful. Think about where you were. What were you doing?* Write these thoughts in your journal.

Caring for your body is greater than curing an illness. Good health means having plenty of energy to do all that you need to do—or want to do. The outcome of how we live our lives eventually are reflected in our bodies. When we get sick, it may indicate that our immune system have become weakened due to being under a great deal of stress. *Why take your health for granted?* As you minimize your energy drains, you'll experience that taking good care of your body will get increasingly easier. Work towards making your health a priority before sickness strikes. *Until then, is there one simple change you can make now to improve your physical health?* Write that change in your journal.

Relationships

The relationships you share with significant people in your life, are probably the most important ingredients of a holistic, high-quality life. These relationships mold and shape who you are and bring meaning to your life. *How often have you put relationships on hold while you were pre-occupied doing something else?* Particularly doing it time and time again, takes a toll and may eventually damage a relationship. Know that it's never too late to rebuild a relationship that is important to you. When you have a strong relationship, it enriches your life and empowers you with a sense of security. When it is weak, you feel drained of energy whether you realize it or not.

What relationships you have not nurtured? How are the people you haven't seen in a while? Don't wait for trouble to surface. Review the following list to determine if there is a relationship that needs some attention. Write the names in your journal.

Parents   *Friends*
Mate   *Neighbors*
Children   *Co-Workers*
Extended Family

Leisure/Recreational

Building leisure and fun into your life on a regular basis will help you to relax from the seriousness in life, and more importantly, will create memories that you will relish for a lifetime. Remember a time in which you're having fun, it is just as important as your time spent working. *What have you done for recreation lately?*

Write your ideas in your journal.

Work

The quality of your work life is specifically related to the level of happiness you derive for your career. Everyone may have different needs when it relates to their careers; the quality level of their work life is impacted by whether those needs are being met.

Those with a high quality of work life generally make enough to live comfortably, find their work to be interesting or engaging, and achieve a level of personal satisfaction or fulfillment from the jobs that they do. In other words, employees who are generally happy with their work are said to have a high quality of work life, and those who are unhappy or unfulfilled by their work are said to have a low quality of work life.

Then there is what the literature refers to as "*work-life ba*lance." "Work-life balance" is somewhat misleading. It does not mean an equal balance like trying to schedule an equal number of hours for each of your various work and personal activities – family, friends, etc. It's a misnomer and it can set you up for failure. "Work-life balance" implies that if you spend a set amount of time in your work, you'll have to spend that same amount of time on whatever else makes up your life – personal time, physical fitness, family, parenthood, hobbies, etc. Basically, everything that is important to you – work and the rest of your life – is split between two opposite ends of the spectrum.

They're either/or. Trying to do this is usually unrewarding and unrealistic. Life actually flows. Life is and should be more fluid.

Did you know that your best individual work-life balance will vary over time? It often does on a daily basis! The right balance for you today may be different for you tomorrow. The right balance for you when you have children, may be different when you're single with children or if you're married with children. Your balance may be different when you have a non-career job—when you start a new career—or, when you're transitioning towards retirement.

There is no perfect, one-size fits all balance that you should be striving for. The best work-life balance is different for each of us because we all have different priorities and different lives. The reality though is that it is more of an ebb and flow, than reaching balance.

Work/Career Satisfaction

The thing(s) that would make me feel more satisfied in my work/career is/are:

_____

_____

_____

_____

As I envision what it would be like to have my work/career exactly as I want, the following would be evident:

_____

_____

_____

_____

The thing(s) that I might be fearful of or hesitate to change are:

_____

_____

_____

_____

(Note: Downloadable blank form on www.HaveJoyLLC.com)

Self-Exploration:

Coaching

Looking at the answers to the previous listed questionnaires, including your Professional and Personal Inventory, what you love doing, what drains your energy, and clarifying your values.

Write a statement that summarizes where you want to go or make progress towards in your life.

_____

_____

_____

_____

(Note: Downloadable blank form on www.HaveJoyLLC.com)

Look at the lists that were presented earlier in this chapter to see whether you have considered all of your possible directions. Coaching may be a good fit for you as you consider your vision, the goals to manifest your vision, and the action-steps to take to achieve your goals.

"The only place success comes before work,
is in the dictionary."
—Vince Lombardi

Resources

The 28 Laws of Attraction: Stop Chasing Success and Let It Chase You, by Thomas Leonard (New York: Scribner, 2007).

> Provides an excellent template for manifesting energy to become more attractive and drawing your destiny towards you.

The Dark Side of the Light Chasers by Debbie Ford (New York: The Berkley Publishing Group, 1999).

> Excellent book that can connect you with addressing energy drains.

The Four Agreements by Don Miguel Ruiz (California: Amber-Allen Publishing, 1997).

> Extremely helpful book in illuminating the power of aligning one's integrity.

Values-Based Coaching-A Guide for Social Workers and Other Human Service Professionals by Marilyn Edelson (District of Columbia: National Association of Social Workers, 1997-2015).

> In this book on coaching specifically for social workers, it gives voice to the social work profession on a controversial topic that presents tremendous opportunities for bringing about positive change. Health care and human service professionals in other disciplines will also benefit from its theoretical grounding and practical information on coaching with diverse clientele.

Your Best Year Yet! Ten Questions for Making Your Next Twelve Months Your Most Successful Ever by

Jinny Ditzler (New York: Warner Books, 2000).
 Provides an amazing personal strategic planning process that aligns your core values with your personal purpose, mission, and life roles.

CHAPTER 2

Achieve a Clear Vision

"The future never just happened, it was created."
-Will and Ariel Durant

Steps Toward Joy

1. Define your personal vision and describe your vision statement.
2. Define your personal mission and describe your mission statement and its purpose.
3. Describe SMART goals and how they support your vision and mission.

****

Defining a Vision

Your vision is the guiding theme of your professional career and personal life. It is a long-term image that creates your priorities and choices for making short-term decisions. Your vision is a vivid description (a reference point to guide your decisions, planning, and actions for the future). Your vision evolves out of your values, as introduced in the previous chapter. Webster's New Collegiate Dictionary defines vision as "*something seen otherwise than by ordinary sight; something beheld as in a dream."*

Some people have asked: *"Why have a vision? Does it really matter?"* The answer is that a vision provides direction for your life and the context for your decisions. If you don't know where you are going – any road can lead you off-course. To lead people, or even to lead in your own personal life, you need to know where you want to go. Vision motivates you to perform to your potential and beyond. A vision reduces the possibility of becoming complacent.

Your strong and clear vision also has the power to make you a role model. When your family, friends, co-workers or employees see that you have a clearly defined vision in your life and career, they will want to imitate you. As a leader, you will be admired and your vision will provide the framework and context not only for your decisions, but also for the directives that you give - and the work that you may ask them to perform.

Many people and organizations have found it helpful to reflect their vision as a vision statement. Doing this forces you to ask yourself some profound questions:

What should your vision statement say?
What are the most important things in your life?
What do you want to achieve?
What do you want to be known for?

Your vision should include what matters most to you. When you write your vision statement, you need to clarify your values and reflect upon them. Think about the words that best express who you aspire to be.

Your priorities will shift as you gain varied experiences, get older, advance in your career or, maybe even change careers. That's why you should consider your vision statement as something that's fluid; a living document, something that can and will change over time. It is not carved in stone! In fact, don't be surprised if you revisit your statement, reassess your priorities, and make changes every couple of years.

Successful people have one trait in common, and that is clarity. They need to be clear about what they want and what they want to accomplish. It's that laser focus that helps them determine what actions to take and where to spend their energy on a daily basis. Being clear as a leader in your life and in the workplace means being simple, exact, and understandable. You constantly bring the most important things to light, be it current reality and/or future possibility.

Success stories about life achievements in our personal and professional endeavors highlight the idea that with a vision in mind, you are more likely to succeed beyond what you would otherwise not achieve without a clear vision. Take a moment and consider that developing your life vision is plotting a course to your personal and professional dreams. Your joy and happiness is within reach. However, if you don't develop and explore your vision, you are more at risk of circumstances and other people directing the course of your life.

"Life isn't about finding yourself.
Life is about creating yourself."
-George Bernard Shaw

Our life is a creation. Our life is a gift that we can shape as we please. However, as we go about our day being busy "creating" experiences in our life, do we begin with a clear vision of the work of art that we're trying to create? Can we visualize our product? Or, is our life so harried and rushed that we are aimlessly adding pieces to our quilt-work of life, hoping something might just naturally fall into place?

We've all had experiences like that, just taking life as it comes. Depending on which stage of life we're in, we may find ourselves focusing so much on our current events that we seem unaware of the long-term. We've got nothing but time, right? Well, we all live in the present and try to deal with things as they affect us in the present. However, expanding our vision leads to addressing the entire circle of life and not just a slice of the pie. In fact, let's think of baking a pie. Before you begin to bake, you have an idea of how you would like the pie to look and taste. You know what type of pie you're baking, you've got the pie's recipe, and you know how much time it should take. So, if you try to create the life that you want without identifying the actions to take, you'll live frequently falling short of your dreams. In fact, it may leave you with a bad taste in your mouth! If you fail to plan, you can plan to fail.

*"If the leader and people in an organization
think the company is small, they will act that way.
If they think the company is big, they will act that way."*
–David J. Greer

Coach's Reflection - Mark

Mark, a high school principal shared an example
wherein his personal vision was connected with
making a difference – cognitively, affectively, socially,
and physically – for every student. Student success
was at the heart of his vision. He entered a school
where patterns of behavior and unwritten rules
protected seniority in the organization as a core value.
Veteran teachers were assigned advanced placement
classes and the best schedules, whereas newcomers
were frequently assigned struggling students with
learning challenges and less desirable schedules.
He reflected, "I knew I had to work hard to remove this
misalignment. I knew what I encountered was what I
didn't want, but this situation made me aware that I
had to come up with a detailed vision of what I wanted
if I was to be successful. I had to make this picture so
attractive that it would generate followers – so I
wouldn't be the only one sharing … or living this
vision!"

"Success comes from within, not from without."
—Ralph Waldo Emerson

Optimism is heightened by a well-developed vision
that everyone's excited about. People become energetic
and they begin to see the possibilities. Ideally, they are
so enthused that they forget their fears or limiting

thinking. A vision helps to stretch, to inspire, and to motivate. Living the vision is a necessity in accomplishing the vision.

Coach's Reflection - Sheila

Sheila, a principal of a campus of approximately 1,500 students who decided that the most important part of the job at the beginning of the year was to enforce the dress code. This principal advised the teachers that part of first period homeroom should begin with assessing students' dress code – and that any non-compliant students should be sent to the office to be disciplined. Nearly 1/4th of the students were sent to the office the first day. Administrative personnel's morning was consumed by Discipline Referrals and processing students to be sent home. This continued to happen every day for three weeks, at which point, the leadership team decided that the dress code could not be enforced. So, the dress code was relaxed and then perceived as having been dropped. Of course, the students felt that they won! Ultimately, student behavior declined and became a larger problem. Fights were occurring. Some bomb threats were being called in, and while outside waiting for the building to be cleared for safety, students were leaving campus (cutting school). The school was becoming an out of control, unsafe environment.

This story can be contrasted with that of another school principal's experience. Each year, this principal goes to each language arts class and spends time talking to the students about their expectations and answering questions that the

---

students may have. This principal also invites the students to talk to her when they need to. The principal establishes a relationship of respect with the students, and is very clear about expectations and consequences for actions. This school functions well.

Visualizing a detailed image of the future creates an image in our minds that we can see and relate to. Our mind conceives in pictures. Our mind doesn't know if the picture in the mind is real, a dream, or simply a wish. In the left side of the brain, our conscious mind, we think about the future and the ways in which we can achieve goals in the future. Unfortunately, it's in our conscious mind that we can talk ourselves out of our goals. Our internal dialogue says things such as, "It costs too much," "I can't possibly do this," and "I'm too old to be trying something new." These are only a few of the limiting messages our conscious mind can create as we consider new goals. It stops forward movement and prevents accomplishing the goal.

However, in the right side of the brain, within our subconscious mind, exists our dreams and the opportunity to explore new and unlimited possibilities. Our emotions are processed by the right side of the brain. It compels us when we are driven to want to make a change. The visualization, a powerful process, enables us to maintain a visual image, a picture to keep us emotionally connected to the goals we seek to fulfill.

A great deal has been researched about the brain and how it functions. It has been discovered that we've been gathering images since we were born, making interpretations about them and storing them in the subconscious.

Coach's Reflection - Mary:

Mary is a married mother of three who is going to school part-time to complete her degree, a long-held goal, while raising her family and supporting her husband. Her husband, who is a nurse, is on-call twenty-four hours a day for four days straight and rotates off for three days. Mary says her life feels like it's not what she expected. Between school, her kids' activities, and taking care of her home, she lives in a constant state of feeling exhausted most of the time. Her brain stores the image of her family not working, as if it happened and is real. That's pretty powerful.

On the other hand, using visualization techniques, Mary can imagine her family as successful. She sees her husband as supportive in his work ethic and commitment to his family. She visualizes her children

regarding their mother as valuing education and regarding their parents' partnership as preparing for the family's future. When we see it as possible, we tend to create it.

Your vision serves as a compass, lending direction to your behavior. When the vision is one person's vision, but is not embraced by your organizational members (for example, your family or co-workers), individuals may go through the motions or act on *"shoulds"* rather than a deep commitment to that vision. At the heart of any vision is a set of core values and beliefs. You may sometimes experience conflict between your own values, beliefs, and vision for your life, and those of your family or your organization and their existing values, beliefs, and vision. These existing beliefs and values may be reflected, as some people say, as "the way we do things around here."

> *"The most pathetic person in the world*
> *is someone who has sight but no vision."*
> — Helen Keller

There's a certain magical, magnetic quality about people that communicate their vision well. They inspire and attract others – and even better, they attract help. If you can articulate your vision with passion and conviction, you'll be amazed at how easy it is to enlist people into helping you accomplish your goal. That translates into the ability to successfully launch your dreams faster.

It's important to note that achieving clarity of vision is a continual process; it's not something you do only in the initial phase. For leaders and organizations to evolve, there must be a continual evaluation and evolution of the vision as the leader and the organization changes and grows.

Clarifying the vision is about reflecting on the past as much as projecting into the future. Clarifying the vision requires careful consideration of your strengths and limitations. Clarifying the vision is as much about identifying the vision, as it is about the methods of achieving your goals. Clarity prepares you to take action and it enhances your motivation to do what is needed. When you clearly visualize the outcome you want in vivid detail, and really feel how it feels, it's hard not to get excited about taking action!

Draft Your Personal Vision Statement:

_____

_____

_____

_____

(Note: Downloadable blank form on www.HaveJoyLLC.com)

Good leaders must be focused and consistent. It propels them to achieve their goals in a way that followers can depend and count on. I've thought about a personal mission statement years ago. The idea originated in Stephen Covey's book about highly successful people. His idea motivated hundreds of thousands of people to write a personal mission statement. It connects with a powerful idea – begin with the end in mind. If you aspire to be successful in your own life, to be a respected leader who accomplishes good things and empowers those in your life to do likewise, it's prudent to have a roadmap and perspective of how to get there! With clarity about your destination, your focus is able to shift to building the path to achieve and to assess the end product – your results.

Writing a Personal Mission Statement

Personal mission statements are designed for providing a sense of purpose that guides who you want to be and what you want to do. It's a description that encompasses your own personal objectives, long-term goals, and guiding philosophy – all of which impacts your personal and professional lives. In a corporate or institutional environment, a mission statement is a description of what an organization wants to accomplish in business. Similarly, your own mission statement should embrace your personal and professional goals – and the best goals come from what *motivates* you!

What Motivates You? (Circle those that apply)	
Money	Self-satisfaction
Recognition	Desire to please
Fear of failure	Self-worth
Physical needs	Sense of accomplishment
Others?	Faith

After reflecting on your values and your motivations, you will be able to craft your mission statement with more ease. Remember, your mission statement is not supposed to be the Ten Commandments of your life! It should project three to five years into your future. Just like with your vision, revisit your mission statement, reflect upon it, and adjust it as your life changes – because it will evolve and change!

Personal mission statements may need to change as well, particularly when moving into other positions and the goals you aspire to achieve begin to take on new meaning. Think of the personal mission statement as your guide, signs along the side of the road. It's about creating a solid foundation for long-term career and personal goals. I think of it as markers along the journey that we travel that keeps us on the right path when we may face a hard choice or a disappointing setback. It may help you to say "no" when that's the best decision. Just as you will do with your vision, you should revisit your mission statement and adjust it as your life circumstances change.

Here's an example of a possible mission statement that supports a vision statement: *"During the next few years of college, I want to achieve excellent grades (B+ or higher) in all my coursework. I will also seek experience in a leadership role in a committee or activity, and I will actively seek internships, networking opportunities, and other hands-on experience. In addition, I will volunteer in at least one community service organization on a regular basis."*

Notice anything? The mission statement takes the aims of the vision statement and makes them more concrete. The tone of the mission statement is confident and determined. Do any of the aims expressed in this mission statement seem unreasonable or unreachable? Now, you try it!

Draft Your Personal Mission Statement:

_____

_____

_____

_____

(Note: Downloadable blank form on www.HaveJoyLLC.com)

"Leadership is not a magnetic personality — that can just as well be a glib tongue. It is not 'making friends and influencing people'. Leadership is lifting a person's vision to higher sights, the raising of a person's performance to a higher standard, the building of a personality beyond its normal limitations."

–Peter Drucker

Writing SMART Goals to Support a Vision and Mission

To bring your vision to life and accomplish your personal mission, you need to do one more thing: set some definite **goals**. Goals are the things that you set out to do or achieve, short or long term, to fulfill your vision and realize your mission. Begin by thinking of your vision and mission as your life *strategy,* and your goals as the *objectives* that will help you work within and toward that strategy.

Think of your goals as the lines you connect to create the picture described by your vision and mission. Your goals become the *short-term milestones* that will keep you on track and help you achieve your greater mission.

> **S.M.A.R.T.** Goals:
> **S**pecific
> **M**easurable
> **A**ttainable
> **R**ealistic
> **T**ime bound

But how can you write effective goals? One technique is to write SMART goals. SMART goals have built-in features that help you attain them. They are specific, measurable, attainable, realistic, and time bound. Here's an example of how to write a SMART goal.

If your vision is to be a successful entrepreneur and your mission, in support of that, is to attain excellent grades in pursuing your college degree, how exactly do you get there? A SMART goal that implements those vision and mission statements might be to *get an 'A' in business math this semester by joining and regularly attending a study group by the third week of the term.* Notice how the goal sets a specific measurable benchmark and an attainable deadline. If you find that helpful, you can then write goals for each of your classes or activities to ensure forward movement.

The final step in this process is to prioritize your SMART goals. Put your goals in the order of importance, time required to complete the goal, overall attainability, cost, any outside help that will be needed, or any other resource needed in order to organize them. Organize your time and effort. Don't randomly list your goals, as it may waste your time and effort. Whether you decide to accomplish your small stuff first and the more challenging ones later – or vice versa – is up to you, but you must *organize* your time and the effort you devote to your goals.

Developing a personal vision statement, mission statement, and SMART goals are key steps in developing your identity as an adult and leader in your own life. Visions, missions, and goals will help bring out the best qualities of your personality and make you a desirable role model for your loved ones, co-workers, and your subordinates in the future. You never know the extent of your potential until you reach it — and then step further. A clear vision, a specific mission, and definite goals are important tools that will help you reach, and even exceed your very own expectations.

Coaching Questions toward A Vision and Mission

-Think of a time when you, a staff member, or a group resisted a change. What was the root of it?

-You may have noticed limiting beliefs expressed by your social circle or co-workers. How can you begin to shift a limiting belief to grow into a positive belief?

Resources

Decoding Your Destiny by Carmen Harra, Ph.D. (Oregon: Atria Books/Beyond Words, 2006).

This book presents your soul code, a means by which you can see who you truly are, understand your destiny, and use your free will to make the most of your potential. With your soul code in hand, you'll learn about the tool of prediction: the more you think on a specific potentiality, predict it, and put your intentions to work, the more likely it is you'll achieve it. Combining intention with action is the practice of manifestation and free will.

Leaders: The Strategies for Taking Charge by Warren G. Bennis and Burt Nanus (New York: Harper Business Book, 1985).

In this illuminating study of corporate America's most critical issue – leadership – these co-authors reveal the four key principles every manager should know: Attention Through Vision, Meaning Through Communication, Trust Through Positioning, and The Deployment of Self. In this age of "process," with downsizing and restructuring affecting many workplaces, companies have fallen trap to lack of communication and distrust, and vision and leadership are needed more than ever before.

Leadership Coaching for Educators by Karla Reiss (California: Corwin Press, 2007).

This resource gives school leaders tools and techniques for designing and implementing a successful coaching program that creates long-lasting educational change.

My American Journey by Colin Powell (New York: Random House, 1995).

Insights shared pertaining to successful military leaders attaining greatness not by luck, but by having values, goals, vision, and a sense of mission.

Take Time for Your Life by Cheryl Richardson (New York: Broadway Books, 1998).

This book offers an inspiring, practical, seven-step program to help you create the life you want.

The Shaping School Culture Fieldbook by Kent Peterson and Terrence Deal (San Francisco: Jossey-Bass, 2002).

This book shares new ideas and strategies on how stories, rituals, traditions, and other cultural practices can be used to create positive, caring, and purposeful schools. It gives expanded attention to the important symbolic roles of school leaders, including practical suggestions on how leaders can balance cultural goals and values against accountability demands, and features new and powerful case examples throughout. Most importantly, the authors show how school leaders can transform negative and toxic cultures so that trust, commitment, and sense of unity can prevail.

Online Resource

https://training.tonyrobbins.com/4-steps-to-creating-the-ultimate-vision-for-your-life/
   "4-Steps to Creating the Ultimate Vision for Your Life" by Anthony Robbins.

CHAPTER 3

What Do You Really Want?

*"The moment you learn to separate
your wants from your needs,
your vision becomes clearer."*
— Kemi Sogunle

Steps Toward Joy:

1. Focus and think about what you *want*, not on what you *don't want*.
2. Focus on your wishes, not what others dictate for you.
3. Know that you have permission to dream. Dreaming is not just for children!

****

Having a vision is something intangible until you act upon it and bring it to life. It should include addressing the five key areas of our lives: Spiritual, Emotional/Physical, Work Relationships, and Leisure. You must determine what you need to do to make consistent progress toward living the life you've envisioned. So, what do you want? This will involve creating a set of prioritized goals so that you can spend your time getting the results that you want.

This question sounds like a trick, but it is often very hard to answer. Giving yourself time to investigate your deeply held hopes and dreams can be very scary. You may also think that you've been blessed already and you shouldn't have to think of "pursuing one more thing." Don't you have enough already? You don't have enough time in the day to think about one more thing that you want out of life. Yet, it's important to remind yourself that a fulfilled life usually happens by purposeful design.

I believe that we're all here for a reason, a purpose. Although at different stages in our lives our purpose may change and evolve, we all have significance in the world. We are all blessed with unique talents and gifts. How we express those gifts and manifest them in the world, is an expression that contributes to a greater cause than our mere selves.

For the last several years, I was operating on high energy, limited rest, and unlimited potential in pursuit of what I considered to be the ultimate goal of education, prestige, and the elusive success. Along the way, I met "Sharon" (not her real name). "Sharon" had succeeded in reaching her financial goals; being a leader in her industry; and obtaining a beautiful home, elite cars, and the ability to afford the finest things that money could buy. She nurtured a family with her spouse and they raised three children. Through her diligence and hard work, "Sharon" made it and she had it all! However,

"Sharon" wasn't happy; in fact, she felt unfulfilled. When she reflected and explored further, she realized that she did not have the time to enjoy the wealth she helped to create for her family. She wanted joy and peace. She wanted to not just endure or maintain her life, but to actively live her life. She, regrettably, was not able to. She had too many responsibilities, too much to protect …. or too much to lose. Her personal relationships were becoming strained because her focus and energy were not as directed towards her relationships. Her priorities reflected where she spent the most time, and it was becoming painfully clear that her family was being sacrificed. She was on a treadmill. However, instead of losing weight, she was gaining weight from stress-eating and losing in her relationships.

As I grew to know "Sharon", my own experience was illuminated. Her reflection propelled me towards clarity that I could be her. I had a comfortable lifestyle, but lacking in time devoted towards the relationships in my life. Here I was in my mid-life, and I did not want to spend the next ten to twenty workable years chasing after titles and money at the expense of becoming bankrupt spiritually, emotionally, physically, and mentally. What was I chasing? I had to slow down. I devoted my time from 2013 through 2015 to re-assessing my purpose and that which brought joy to my life. I began to look more closely at my life and asked myself, "If this was my last day, what would matter most to me?" I secured a Coach. Me? A person who was used to having the answers and being in control? This revelation caused me to look at my own life vision and decide whether what I was doing aligned with my values and goals. I was one of the lucky ones because I was blessed to work in education with dedicated professionals to impact the lives of children. We were making our own imprint on the future. However, with there being only 24-hours in a day for all of us (I was not special to have more allotted time than others!), what I did with the non-work hours was significant to living a fulfilled life. I felt as though I was living to work.

The vision is all about where you want to go. The mission is how you're going to get there. As I clarified the vision for my life, I decided that whatever opportunities I was willing to commit to, they must be aligned with my values, goals, and life's mission. After deep reflection and inner-work, I developed the following in my preparation for moving forward:

Here is my vision statement:
To think different. To be different. To make a difference.

Here is my mission statement:
To inspire joy through teaching and guidance.
To help people stop avoiding their dreams in life and get busy creating them.

Here are some of my values:
-I value being connected spiritually.
-I value the importance of family.
-I value having meaningful relationships.

Here are some of my goals:
-To have control of my time and venue. I look forward to working only on projects that I connect with.

-I plan to secure resources without compromising my values, goals, and personal mission.
-To travel and experience different cultures.
-To live every day joyfully!

And this vision and mission now guide the work I do every day in an inspirational and positive way.

"Knowing what you don't want in life is almost as helpful as having a five year plan. Vision doesn't always mean you know exactly what you want to do or where you want to be in life; sometimes, vision is knowing where you don't want to be in order to find where you should end up!"

— Amanda Bernardo

Coaching Questions to Clarify What You Want:

As you prepare for self-reflection, you may find it helpful to write your thoughts in a journal or notebook. The following is a list of questions that can assist you in discovering your purpose as you work towards tapping into your vision. These questions are intended to guide you into defining your own personal mission. Feel free to explore further by adding your own questions. You may ask others what they want out of life. You may find it interesting to set your answers aside and then come back to them at a later time to see if any have changed, or if you've decided to add to them.

1. *Spiritual*
-What issues do you care about?
-What would you most like to accomplish?
-What legacy would you like to leave behind?

2. *Emotional/Physical*
-What qualities would you like to develop within yourself?
-What would bring more joy and happiness into your life?

3. *Work*
-What are your dreams and secret passions?
-If money was not an issue, what would you want in your career?

4. *Relationships*
-What really matters to you in life? (What *does* matter, not what *should* matter.)
-What do you want your relationships to look like?

5. *Leisure*
-What would you like to have more of in life?
-What activity brings you a sense of peace?
-What activity, if any, gives you an adrenaline rush? Perhaps a memory from your childhood or adolescence.

Now try to clarify the following for yourself:

My personal vision statement is

_____

_____

My personal mission statement is

_____

_____

Some of my values are

_____

_____

_____

_____

Some of my goals are

_____

_____

_____

_____

Coaching clients may come from many different walks of life, but they have a common element in that they desire something more – more purpose and meaning, more money or business, more passion for what they are doing in their life, or a heightened desire to make a difference. Often, a life change may have prompted them to take action – a job anniversary, marriage, divorce, milestone birthday, a job transition (layoff, demotion, or promotion), or an inspiration from someone else's life (such as a book or a movie).

Coach's Reflection - Michael

Michael, a Certified Public Accountant, was unhappy with his CPA business. The long hours were no longer compatible with this stage of his life or with his family values. He was becoming resentful of his work and the lack of career progress that he was experiencing. He did not see himself as going into business for himself. Through the coaching partnership, he was encouraged to assess his whole life and to do a life planning exercise with his wife. Within months, it became increasingly clear that they both shared a vision of travelling. It did not take Michael long to find a new position. The family relocated and are much happier now.

Other coaching clients may have a "dilemma" that they're concerned about resolving. They may feel that they are performing adequately at work or that their job is no longer a good fit for them—or perhaps it hasn't been for quite a while. Many coaching clients are "stuck." They don't consider themselves as having mental health issues, but they are aware that they have hit a wall and need help becoming "un-stuck."

Coach's Reflection - Cheryl

Cheryl had hit a wall with her health. Despite being very satisfied with her life, she was unable to lose weight. She was highly motivated, but she lacked – and needed – more accountability. She had joined many different weight loss programs. She was not pleased with their programs and complained that they did not personalize their programs enough for her. What she really wanted was a personal trainer for her health and well-being.

When she began being coached, it was clear that the pattern that led to her weight gain involved more than just food. Cheryl was dealing with a number of personal challenges that drained her of her energy and left her feeling lonely and frustrated, so she ate to compensate for those feelings. Through the coaching partnership, Cheryl was able to develop a systematic plan to eliminate her energy drains.

Coach's Reflection - John

John was an eager coaching client. He was enthusiastic about reaching his performance goals and made weekly progress. John identified one personal goal in addition to his professional goals—to improve his relationship with his son. However, even though it was an important goal for him, he resisted taking action toward it beyond what he'd already tried. In fact, John avoided talking about it. He was fearful that the relationship would get worse in the process. In moving forward, John was willing to take safe, small steps.

During the coaching sessions, a great deal of time was spent talking about John's fears and brainstorming other actions he could take to accomplish his goals. In time, John and his son began enjoying an improved relationship.

Resources

A New Earth: Awakening to Your Life's Purpose, by Eckhart Tolle. (New York: Penguin Group, 2005).
> This book guides you through understanding yourself as a spiritual being having a human experience through life.

Happy Women Live Better, by Valorie Burton (Oregon: Harvest House Publishers, 2013).
> This book presents that women have more education, more money, and more choices than ever before, yet research shows we are less happy than women 40 years ago. Today, we can "have it all." So why is happiness declining? This book unlocks the secret to your personal happiness. It reveals 13 happiness triggers – choices that can boost your joy right now, even in the midst of deadlines, children, marriage, dating, and squeezing in a workout or girls' night out.

Living Your Joy, by Suzanne Falter-Barns. (New York: Random House, 2003).
> This is a funny and practical book that helps you bring clarity to your thinking and master the nitty-gritty of getting from where you are to where you want to be.

The Alchemist, by Paulo Coelho. (New York: Harper Collins, 1993).
> An intriguing fable about pursuing your dreams.

The Secret of the Shadow: The Power of Owning Your Whole Story, by Debbie Ford.　　(San　　　　Francisco: Harper, 2001).

This book shows you how to rediscover your true essence hidden in the shadow of your dramatic life story.

CHAPTER 4

Can There Be Joy At Work?

*"What the mind of man can conceive and believe,
it can achieve."*
–Napolean Hill

Steps Toward Joy:

1. Know that happiness is largely a choice.
2. Find something in your current job to love.
3. Be willing to gain from personal and professional development.

****

If you are not diligently pursuing the activities that bring joy into your life, then you may be missing out on a life that is more fulfilled. There are ways to create a strategy that inspires joy in your work life. In creating a vision for success, Allison Rimm, the author of The Joy of Strategy: A Business Plan for Life, notes in her book to "think big"—something people who are task-oriented and analytical may struggle with doing. However, many home-makers, leaders, business-people, and entrepreneurs have the opposite problem: they may often have great visions and wrestle with conflicting ideas as to how to make these visions happen.

Coach's Reflection - Carol

Carol was working in a position she no longer liked and was considering a change. As a single mother, she was worried about sacrificing the benefits and security she believed she needed. Through her coaching work, she identified a part of herself that she felt was under-utilized – her creativity. She began to recall when she was the most joyous; it was when she was personally creating beautiful things. In previous years, she had created some jewelry and longed for the loving process of creating something beautiful. She regretted that her job wasn't a creative one. We began to coach through the part of her life that she felt was "asleep." Initially, we discarded the idea of her quitting her job and simply focused on her joy. Carol started to make jewelry in her spare time. She wanted to make jewelry to bring to the world to help people have more beauty in their lives. She began to donate the jewelry to the children's wards in local hospitals. Her work was noticed. She received donations to create more jewelry and was featured on a local television news program for her community service. As she brought more joy to her life and to others, she surprised herself by discovering she was much happier at work. Her job was the same. It was *she* who changed!

Our thoughts and behaviors play a significant role in the type of energy that we attract to ourselves. Positive thoughts attract positive energy, and negative thoughts attract negative energy. Both have the power to influence our behavior in ways that impact the way we navigate through life. Toxic, negative habits have the power to take the joy right out of our grasp ... even when the joy was so close we could almost touch it and we could feel the cool breeze that comforted us. As we walk through life, know that we can identify the joy stealers in our lives. We can strengthen our skills to create new habits and activities which may bring more positive energy to us.

"Happiness is there when you have
great imagination and vision,
when you take relentless action and love your creation."
–Debashish Mridha

1. Your happiness at work is a choice.
Choosing to be happy at work is sometimes hard to do, but you can do it, even if you don't have a great boss (if you are self-employed and you are your own boss---work on that!). By focusing positively on the aspects of your job that you like, you will increase your happiness quotient. Seek employees you enjoy and spend time with them while avoiding gossip and negativity.

HOLD ON TO THE JOY-
Solely relying on your work to bring you joy may steal your joy. When being responsible for others, you may find that your own self-care is taking a back seat to your moving forward. However, when you minimize your own self-care, you become overworked, stressed, and ultimately, unhappy.

Eventually, if we don't take care of ourselves, we won't have the physical or emotional resources to take care of others. So make sure that on your calendar (or "To Do" list) you've dedicated time for yourself. Allow time to unwind, sharing experiences with special people and enjoying your favorite hobbies. Regularly rejuvenate yourself and don't feel guilty about it!

2. Develop friendships.
This enables establishing a network that provides resources and care in the work environment.

HOLD ON TO THE JOY-
Striving to be friends with everyone you come into contact with may steal your joy. In particularly distressing cases, friendships can become sour, destructive, and filled with resentment and bitterness. No matter how long you have known someone or how much you have shared together, sometimes the best thing you can do is to go your separate ways.

However, throughout the course of life, many of us are lucky enough to meet a few people along the way who, for some reason or another, we simply "click" with. Perhaps you meet someone who happens to like exactly the same things as you - a love for gospel music or maybe a passion for organic recipes, someone who you can talk to for hours and they practically finish your sentences, or someone who intuitively knows what you're talking about without you having to explain in detail. Or perhaps you have nothing much in common with this person, but you admire their qualities - their positivity, their sense of humor, their easy-going way with people. Sometimes two people can become great friends even when they come from different cultures, have different desires, and have completely different aspirations. Friendship, like love, is built upon a feeling, an instinct that tells us when something is just right.

Although the feeling of friendship usually comes naturally, the development of a long-term friendship requires time, effort, and compromise to become something durable and long-lasting.

3. Embrace Positivity.

Happiness and joy are conscious choices. Participating in gossip, negativity, and engaging with unhappy people should be minimized as much as possible—if not eliminated altogether. Negative people have a significant impact on our emotional and psychological well-being.

HOLD ON TO THE JOY-

Taking things personally steals your joy. When negativity enters your space, try not to take things personally. When someone directs their negative energy towards you, they could be rude, mean, or judgmental. Hold on to the realization that this has more to do with them and less to do with you. They may not be happy. Sometimes it's easier said than done, but don't let the negative behaviors of others get you down and increase the negative energy in your life. Joyful people do not attack.

So find it within yourself to conjure up sympathetic thoughts and move on with your life. We attract more of what we concentrate on, so don't let negativity fill your concentration. Focus on those people and the events that support you instead.

HOLD ON TO THE JOY-
Participating in drama steals your joy. You should avoid participating in any drama that may occur. The way that you may react to an event can actually contribute to a situation becoming more dramatic. While negatively reacting or defending a position may temporarily feel good, it just puts more oil in the fire and may result in an emotional overload. Try demonstrating a more evolved response. Forgive and move on, and you'll ultimately be immensely rewarded. Remember from this experience that there are ways to speak the truth in a positive way that will be better for all those involved.

4. Nurture your growth.

Do not expect others to take a lead in your personal or professional development. If you don't take the lead, you are then responsible for impeding your own growth. After all, you are the person who will benefit, or lose the most from your own development. Your employer can provide insight and guidance from their global perspective. Should you leave your job, you are taking your growth and professional development with you – it cannot be transferred to another employee during your exit interview.

HOLD ON TO THE JOY-

Striving for perfection will steal your joy. It impedes your chances of being happy and experiencing the fullness of joy. Perfection is not real, it is an illusion. We're human and we make mistakes. In fact, show me the person who has never made a mistake, and I'll show you someone who has not yet experienced their highest level of success yet. In fact, some of your mistakes or failures can be some of our greatest growth experiences from which we learn so much about ourselves. Instead of striving for perfection, try striving for excellence instead. You'll feel more energized!

Coach's Reflection - Melissa

Melissa was an executive director of a non-profit organization. With a very small budget, a small staff, and ambitious goals, she felt stretched and over-worked. In addition, there were morale challenges at work and a difficult teenager at home as well as Melissa's desire to lose some weight, and complete her doctoral dissertation she had been plugging through for the past 5 years.

In the coaching process, a list of three goals were created: improve her ability to efficiently address multiple tasks at work, progress through her doctorate, and lose weight. We began to deal with the daily and weekly challenges of each goal individually. Ways in which she could carve out special time each week to focus solely on her dissertation were identified. She was able to incorporate arriving early at the office and learned to say no to distractions. At other times, she forced herself to take a 30-minute uninterrupted lunch break to be able to clear her thoughts. She was able to focus on her health goal and found that by doing so, she had more energy and felt less depleted at work. She learned to strategically communicate with her secretary to empower developing her leadership skills and initiative, thereby minimizing being micromanaged.

By having a clear list of prioritized goals, the coaching partnership supported designing weekly action steps that led to a greater sense of professional and personal accomplishment. By addressing personal and professional goals, Melissa was able to improve several areas of her life.

5. Be informed.

Employees may feel disillusioned about the lack of information that they receive about their organization, initiatives, or fellow employees. You should not wait and rely on your employer to close the gap of your knowledge. Be active in your own acquisition of knowledge. Develop and participate in a professional network. You may desire to have monthly meetings with your employer to keep the lines of communication open to support your learning. There is only one person in charge of the information that you receive and apply to your life—and that's you.

HOLD ON TO THE JOY-
Lack of necessary information may steal your joy. Holding on to your vision too tightly can steal your joy. Having a large dream with realistic goals and working toward creating your vision is beautiful and important. However, remember that we are not in this alone and that the universal energy is at work also, so it's important to flow as well. It's okay to use an eraser and modify the vision that was written. As we go through different opportunities and seasons in our life, that may be the right thing to do since life is ever-changing. The more information we may have, the more prudent it may be to modify our initial vision.

6. Ask "How Am I Doing?"
Become comfortable with asking your boss for an assessment of your work. Talk to those that you serve as well; if you're providing stellar service, the feedback that you receive will be positive.

HOLD ON TO THE JOY-
Comparing yourself to others may steal your joy. There aren't too many things that can strip you of your strength as quickly as being compared to others. Remember that there is no one else in the universe who is identical to you in being, interests, and desires of the heart. It's a good thing that no

one on Earth has the same strengths and weaknesses. The story that you bring to the world is unique to you and you alone. So, if you notice that someone else is pretty amazing, don't lose your joy through jealousy – although jealousy is a natural emotion. Turn it into a positive by using its existence as evidence to motivate you so that you can manifest your own amazing dream!

7. Do Not Over-Extend Yourself.

Oftentimes, workers find themselves making excuses for not fulfilling a commitment and becoming stressed about the consequences of not keeping that commitment. Once you've developed a systematic approach to planning and organizing your projects and commitments, you'll be able to manage your time more efficiently and fulfill your commitments. Sometimes you may feel that being a "team-player" is key to your career progression; however, you'll do less damage to your career if you don't volunteer when you know that you don't have the time. Don't drown in a sea of unfulfilled commitments. If your workload exceeds your available time and energy, you may have to consider asking your employer for additional resources or to reassess the priorities of the projects.

HOLD ON TO THE JOY-

Excessive technology involvement can steal your joy. It's wonderful to be able to connect with people world-wide as quickly as a stroke of the key or touch of a screen. Used correctly, technology can improve efficiency. However, overuse can rob you of being fully "present" in the current moment. Although social media may add another level of connectedness in your life, make sure that you are incorporating more time into actually *living your own life* rather than watching the lives of others unfold before you online. Your life is important also! Set tech limits for yourself and experience your joy increase!

8. Be Courageous.

Oftentimes, the tough issues are the ones which enable us to grow the most, to be courageous. Yet, it is human nature to want to avoid conflict as it is typically viewed as harboring negative consequences. However, when handled well, conflict can help you reach viable solutions and enable fulfilling your personal vision and overall mission.

HOLD ON TO THE JOY-

Living someone else's dream can steal your joy. Daily, we are influenced by family, co-workers, friends, and society at large. In the midst of all of this, you may experience that your own voice is diminished when listening to the chatter and buzz of all the others. Deep, deep, deep inside of you, there is an inner-voice that whispers knowing what you want to do with your life. That thing in your life that lights the fire in you. This is your life and your time to shine! Be true to yourself and be authentic! Start by asking yourself, "If I only had two years left to live, what would I do if money was not an issue?" Then, consider how many of those things you can actually begin doing now.

The more you are able to do, the happier you will be!

9. Every day is a gift.

Even though every job may have shortcomings, find that "something" in your current job that has a redeeming value to your life. As you examine yourself, you'll experience that if you do something that you enjoy daily, your current job will seem tolerable. In this economy, you always have the option to secure or quit your job.

HOLD ON TO THE JOY-

Not letting the past remain in the past can steal your joy. You are living in the present, and the past is now part of history. Don't go through life reliving things over and over in your mind. Practicing mindfulness can include taking walks, observing nature, or doing yoga or Tai Chi to help you connect with the universal energy around you.

10. When needed, job search with enthusiasm

You don't want to spend your life hating the work that you do. Typically, systematic change in the worksite does not change quickly, only our response to it can occur in a fast time frame. However, for employees who are not happy, their negativity can become pervasive—if not tapped. You may secretly experience peace away from work while pursuing your passion. This may lead you to quit your job to pursue your passion.

HOLD ON TO THE JOY-

Worry can steal your joy. Tomorrow is not

promised. However, we live through our "present" in preparation for what we anticipate to happen next week, next month, or next year. We should definitely plan for the future, but worrying about it may not make it better. Manifest your faith and try to find contentment in what you can do with what you have at this time. Have you noticed that the "future" usually happens anyway? The laws of attraction reflect that everything that happens, occurs in divine order for the greater good. In retrospect, you can probably think of times that were heart-wrenching, but you see the lesson it taught you. Let these memories empower you as you have faith to move forward.

HOLD ON TO THE JOY-
Making life too serious can steal your joy. Life is serious, but sometimes it does not have to be. We're here to learn, make mistakes, and experience happiness alongside others who are also finding their way. Take a breath. Enjoy the scenery as you take this journey. Laugh, savor the experience, and enjoy life!

Creating routines at work is a very effective way to increase performance and productivity. Scheduling activities at the same time each week – meetings, uninterrupted work time, or visits with clients – creates a sense of routine and order that gives your mind a much-needed rest. Setting up regular periods of time when you're not disturbed will give you a chance to get work done without energy-draining distractions.

Other ways to create routines on the job include:
- Taking some time every morning to plan your day rather than just diving in.
- Checking voice mail and/or e-mail at pre-scheduled times throughout the day.
- Scheduling weekly meetings at the same time (this helps employees benefit from the power of routine, too!)
- Giving yourself 20 minutes before you leave the office to wrap up the day's loose ends.

Reinforce your habits in the workplace by keeping track of the positive results in your journal or notebook for at least a month. Joy is all around us and it has the power to inspire our motivation to accomplish things in our life. You just have to stop and notice when joy is evident around you. Recognize the joy when it presents itself. Can you open yourself to the possibilities to address the things that may steal your joy – and instead, *feel* the joy?

Coaching Questions to Manifest Your Joy at Work:

1. Spiritual
-Does the mission or purpose of your organization make you feel that your job is important?
-What is one small change you can make today to have a positive impact?

2. Emotional/Physical

-Do you know, or are you aware of, staff members who feel joy at work?

-Do you feel privileged to work with other people who appear to experience great joy at work?

-How do you demonstrate your own joy in your organization?

-In the last month, have you received praise for doing good work?

-Does your supervisor, or someone at work, seem to care about you as a person?

-Is there someone at work who encourages your development?

-At work, do your opinions seem to count?

3. Work

-How often do you walk through the company/organization and people greet you with a smile with only a few having questions or complaints?

-Do you accomplish a task or project that will actually result in progress for the organization?

-Have you experienced watching a staff member confidently perform in a situation that would have stunted them in earlier days?

-Do you know what is expected of you at work?

-Do you have the materials you need to do your work correctly?

-At work, do you have the opportunity to do what you do best every day?

-In the last six months, has someone at work talked with you about how you're progressing?

-This last year, have you had opportunities at work to learn and grow?

4. Relationships

-Do administrators, CEOs, managers, or clients seek advice and counsel and demonstrate trusting your wisdom and experience to provide confident direction and guidance when needed?

-Do you counsel staff members about returning to school or pursuing training and degrees?

-How does your staff demonstrate pleasure?

-Do visitors tell you that they feel welcomed in your organization?

-In what ways have you observed people form friendships that assisted the organization and added to their work motivation?

-Are your co-workers committed to doing quality work?

5. Leisure

-Do you have a best friend at work?

-What recreational activity, if any, have you enjoyed with your co-workers?

Resources

First, Break All The Rules: What the World's Greatest Managers Do Differently by Marcus Buckingham and Curt Coffman (Kindle Edition: Eighty Twenty Publishing, 2014).

This insightful research study lists and addresses important questions that, when employees answered them positively, their responses were true indicators of whether people were happy and motivated at work.

Get Out of Your Own Way: Overcoming Self-Defeating Behavior, by Mark Goulston, M.D. and Philip Goldberg. (New York: Berkley Publishing Group, 1996).

This book aids you in identifying and successfully dealing with self-sabotage.

Stand Up for Your Life, by Cheryl Richardson. (New York: Free Press, 2002).

A practical guide to help you develop the courage and confidence to make choices that honor your values, needs, and desires.

The Art of Extreme Self-Care by Cheryl Richardson (USA: Hay House, Inc., 2009).

Inspirational handbook that offers you 12 strategies to transform your life one month at a time. It provides a practical, action-oriented chapter that challenges you to alter one behavior that keeps getting you in trouble.

The Joy of Strategy: A Business Plan for Life by
Allison Rimm (Massachusetts: Bibliomotion, Inc.,
2013).
This book guides readers through a step-by-step
program that helps them "find the joy" in their jobs,
businesses, and personal lives. It explores steps to
create visions and plans and to make those visions
come to life.

Online Resources

www.beliefnet.com
Inspiring website that provides a wealth of
inspiration and information on topics that include
spirituality, religion, morality, family, community,
and more.

www.selfgrowth.com
This website is dedicated to providing valuable
insight on personal growth as it relates to
spirituality, health, relationships, success, money,
and so forth.

www.twitter.com/dawngluskin
"Type A-Zen Positive Thinking Personal Growth",
by Dawn Gluskin. Dawn Gluskin is a self-made
entrepreneur turned author and coach who works
with women to help them connect deeply with
their intuition and make a huge impact in the
world. Her signature style of practical business
and life advice mixed in with soulful guidance in a
mind-body-spirit approach to co-creating an

extraordinary life has helped many tap into their own innate wisdom and achieve big dreams.

http://humanresources.about.com/bio/Susan-M-Heathfield-6016.htm

Susan M. Heathfield is a veteran Human Resources Executive. The mission of this site is to provide accurate, thoughtful, forward-looking information for forward-thinking people who wish to stretch their imagination about how people can relate with co-workers and their workplace. Readers who want to share a new vision about these relationships will return frequently to this site. Basic HR and people management information is provided, but the site focuses on forward-looking concepts to challenge the thinking of people in workplaces worldwide.

CHAPTER 5

What Would Your Best Life Look Like?

"The first step toward creating an improved future is developing the ability to envision it. VISION will ignite the fire of passion that fuels our commitment to do WHATEVER IT TAKES to achieve excellence.
Only VISION allows us to transform dreams of greatness into the reality of achievement through human action.
VISION has no boundaries and knows no limits.
Our VISION is what we become in life. "
—Tony Dungy, NFL Superbowl Coach

Steps Toward Joy:

1. Creating a great vision for your life is important for being successful in life.
2. Setting goals in the various areas of your life will help you clarify your priorities and how you live your life each day.

****

Creating a vision for your life impacts these five areas of a holistic life:
1. Spiritual
2. Emotional/Physical
3. Work
4. Relationships

5. Leisure

When you have no vision, you are at risk of having any direction becoming acceptable – even no direction at all. To start finding your vision, you must devote some quiet time. As a coach, I know that for many people, being still and not doing anything can be difficult. It was hard for me also.

Coach's Reflection - Shannon

Shannon was a licensed counselor in a serious financial dilemma. An unexpected divorce and difficult parenting events with her 2 children put her into deep debt. A slump in the local economy where she had her private practice, and her own crisis-ridden life, had created the perfect storm for her near six-figure income to dwindle next to nothing.

When she began being coached, she shared that she worked with a reputable counseling practice and could probably go back there any time. She seemed very surprised when she was asked if she would returning to another reputable counseling practice and work for someone else. She had hoped that as her coach, she would be encouraged to develop a business idea that she had for herself.

When the basic principle was discussed of her having a strong financial foundation, she wept and shared that she knew that, but had convinced herself she "should" follow her dream and it would all work out somehow. She did return as an employee to the counseling practice and worked tirelessly for one year, happily emailing me that she had paid off all of her debts. She is now financially solvent again and has started to work on her dream business in her part-time. As a result, it was worth waiting to implement her idea because the tools available to her online made running a business much easier to do—even in her current part-time pursuits.

As you work toward opening a world of possibilities for your vision, begin by asking yourself, "What would my best life look like?" Sitting still and pondering over questions such as these will help you reach an answer.

A few prompts to start visualizing your best life:
1. *Spiritual*
-What does your ideal day look like?

-Does your best life make you smile and make your heart sing? If it doesn't, dig deeper, dream bigger.

2. *Emotional/Physical*
-How will you feel about yourself?

-What's your state of mind? Happy or sad? Content or frustrated?

-What does your physical body look like? How do you feel about that?

3. *Work*
-What will you have accomplished already?

-What would you be doing?

-How are you dressed?

4. *Relationships*

-What kind of people are in your life? How do you feel about them?

-Where are you? Where do you live? Think specifics: what city, state, or county; type of community; house or an apartment; style; and atmosphere.

5. *Leisure*

-Are you with another person, a group of people, or are you by yourself?

It's important to focus on the outcome. For now, don't think about the process for getting results yet—that comes next. You must give yourself permission to review this vision every day, even if just for a few moments each day. You must keep your vision alive and in the forefront of your mind.

Coach's Reflection - Juliette

Juliette had just quit her job at a local college where she worked as an executive assistant. She wanted to start her own business as a life coach. I was struck by her zest and commitment. Would she be able to do it? The coaching partnership was sustained for a few months, which was all that her budget would allow, and during that time, she launched her business.

Periodically, she would send e-mails, and recently, I was thrilled to learn that she began an online newsletter, 2 blogs, and created a product. When we connected again, she shared that she "was just getting by" for years, but in the last year, after getting certified in coaching, she moved from "being an employee" to "being an entrepreneur." The catalyst was the cancer-diagnosis of her mother and concern about her aging father's well-being. She knew that to make her dream attainable, she needed to make big changes in her life. She knew she wanted to be financially independent and only work from 9:00 a.m.- 2:00 p.m. everyday.

Juliette started to focus on herself and manifesting more self-care into her life. She began getting regular massages, hired a home-cleaning service, invested money in her business, and hired a Virtual Assistant (VA) and a business coach who helped her develop products to support clients in her business. Juliette knew that she had to give herself permission to strategically position herself in her field to provide a service to her niche, working with female entrepreneurs. She embraced her learning curve and began actively building an online community using Facebook and Twitter. She immediately saw it begin to generate interest in her services. Best of all, Juliette found that she is able to be authentic in aligning her professional life with her personal life according to her values.

Moving forward with the end in mind:

1. Spiritual
-What's the most important choice you would've had to make?
-What beliefs would you have needed to change in what you envisioned in your best life?

2. Emotional/Physical
-What's the last thing that would have to happen to achieve your desired emotional state in your best life?
-What's the last thing that would have to happen to achieve your desired physical condition in your best life?

3. Work
-What would you have needed to learn along the way?
-What important actions would you have had to take?
-What milestones would you have needed to reach along the way for your work status in your best life?

4. Relationships
-What type of support would you have had to enlist?
-How long will it have taken you to realize your best life with your current chosen relationships?

5. *Leisure*

-What habits or behaviors would you have had to cultivate?

> *"It is through vision that innovation is conceived; through will power it is then materialized."*
> —Wayne Chirisa

It's time to consider your first step and the next step that follows. Consider the space between where you are now and where you aspire to be in the future. It may appear impossible, but it is achievable if you approach it one step at a time. Anything that's accomplished in life requires the first step to be taken.

Coach's Reflection - Phoebe

Phoebe was a guidance counselor with her heart set on becoming an assistant principal. Although she felt confident in her ability to successfully do the job, she realized that the route to becoming an assistant principal was not typically from the guidance office, and she thought that would be an obstacle to her being competitive. She desperately wanted to overcome her feelings of uncertainty. Phoebe was so sure that she would not be competitive in reaching her goal to be offered an assistant principal position.

As her coach, my intention was to help her negotiate the obstacles and reach her goal. Within our partnership, we set out to create a plan. Through the

---

coaching process and Phoebe's willingness to take action, she ultimately achieved her goal at the school that she had hoped to serve in. The following are some actions that were taken:

-Creating a personal mission statement that reflected her purpose beyond herself.

-Creating a clear description of her ideal work at her ideal school.

-Interviewing several principals and assistant principals in different grade levels to get a more accurate picture of the position and determine if it was aligned with her personal life mission.

-Contacting the principal at the school she hoped to work in for an informal conversation.

-Interviewing for the position and determining whether or not it was a match for her purpose.

Phoebe learned what would be acceptable for her and what would not be. Although she declined the position because it was not an ideal match to her skill-set, what she elaborated in the interview to move the school forward, the position was shifted to be more in alignment with Phoebe's goals and passions. The result was a productive union between Phoebe and her new school—a great success story!

It's critical to come back to this vision periodically. It won't be surprising when your answers to the questions, your clear picture, and the resulting plans need to change and evolve. This can be very good as you begin to grow in unexpected ways. The best life that you've created a vision for, will evolve and change as well. However, for now, it's important to trust the process, develop your vision, and take your initial step toward making your vision a reality.

Coaching Questions to Envision Your Best Life:

A coach is skilled at providing you with tools to understand and clarify your vision for your personal and professional life. A coach also has the skill set to guide you in embracing your authentic self and finding your life purpose for this season in your life. No longer should you defer your dreams. This is your life. This life is not a theatrical performance and it is not a dress rehearsal ... this is it!

1. ***Spiritual***
   -What do you want to be remembered for? Is there some sort of legacy you want to leave? This can be the start of your vision.

   > *Write down your thoughts and review it several times.*

   -What would you like to do to make your/the world a better place?

   > *Visions usually have a greater dimension to them. You might think that it's impossible for you to fulfill your vision by yourself because of how grand your vision is. Your fulfillment will come from noticing that you*

are a part of the world at large, and with others, you are making your vision materialize and come into being.

2. Emotional/Physical

-What does your ideal life look like in terms of health and wellness?

If you can answer this one, you have the beginning of your vision. Try putting your thoughts down on paper and come back to them daily to create a profile.

-What do you need to do to feel complete (feeling most like your authentic self)?

Depending on how large your vision is, it may require that you work only on a piece at a time.

-Identify the piece that you are drawn to?

This may be the area where the purpose of your life, is at a crossroads with your vision.

-Who must you be to feel fulfilled, satisfied, and happy?

If it's hard for you to answer this question, think about all of the work that you have done (home-life, paid, volunteer).

-Where/when were you the most fulfilled, satisfied, and happy? Who was that person you were then?

This can be the authentic you. If you don't know right now, you may want to consider asking other people in your life who were in those situations. Again, this may be a part of your life purpose.

3. Work

-What skills do you enjoy that you are really good/talented at?

It is possible that in your ideal life, you will want to use these skills. If you would, make sure to note that as well.

-What skills do you enjoy that you want to get better at?

Your vision can have skills that you are not proficient at, but enjoy. You may just need to practice these skills more or determine a way to improve your abilities. Your vision is there to help you make good and viable choices. If you have something that you want to improve upon, then make choices that will enable you to practice that skill.

4. *Relationships*

- What exists in your life that you want to let go of to make room for more of what is good? What do you want less of in your life? Write this down as part of your vision.

5. *Leisure*

-What do you want more of in your life to experience during leisure time? What is so good in your life that you want more of it?

This could be a piece of your vision, so just write it down.

-What types of activities do you enjoy to the extent that you know that you will never tire of them?

Your activities may or may not be a part of your vision. Decide for yourself.

TIP ☺ >>> Create a Vision Board!

The "vision board" is a concept made popular in the self-help book "The Secret." Its purpose is to provide images of your hopes and goals. As you reflect on the images that represent your dreams, it's believed that the universe will respond and bring to you that which you want the most. Whether or not you believe in the "miraculous" nature of the vision board, making your dreams more concrete through imagery is a great way to keep focused toward achieving the future you desire.

The vision board is typically a poster or bulletin board on which you paste images that inspired you and that you've torn from various magazines. There are digital versions of the vision board available that helps you easily create a vision board screensaver. "Digital Post-it Notes" from 3M is a handy piece of software that allows you to create sticky notes on your computer desktop as well as create memo boards and virtual bulletin boards. Check out www.picmonkey.com and www.canva.com for photo editing options that are user friendly for my fellow non-techies!

Resources

Feel the Fear and Do It Anyway: Dynamic Techniques for Turning Fear, Indecision, and Anger into Power, Action, and Love (8-CD set), by Susan Jeffers, Ph.D (2007).
>This CD set helps you become more powerful in the face of your fears.

Life is Not a Stress Rehearsal, by Loretta LaRoche. (New York: Broadway Books, 2001).
>This book provides a great way to reduce stress and have humor, while seriously reconsidering your priorities.

Self Matters: Creating Your Life From Inside Out, by Philip C. McGraw (New York: Simon & Schuster, 2001).
>This book challenges you to find your "authentic self" – that person you once were before life over-extended you.

The Portable Coach: 28 Surefire Strategies for Business and Personal Success, by Thomas J. Leonard, with Byron Larson. (New York: Scribner, 1998).
>This resource offers you 28 ways to shape your life, career, and relationships so that they're satisfying and profitable.

Online Resources

www.ted.com

TED is an amazing website where great thinkers and doers gather and share for inspiration.

www.valorieburton.com

This official website is inspiring and its innovative author and life coach, Valorie Burton, offers resources and training based on the tenets of Positive Psychology.

CHAPTER 6

Creating a Larger Vision for Your Life

"When I dare to be powerful,
to use my strength in the service of my vision,
then it becomes less and less important
whether I am afraid."
—Audre Lorde

Steps Toward Joy:

1. Identify what puts a smile on your face and embrace that which you are passionate about. This is your joy!
2. Through creating your powerful vision for your life, you should keep your purpose ever-present in everything that you do. Ignite passion and enthusiasm in your life.
3. Use clear images of the future vision you will create. Focus only on what you want to create versus what you don't want to create.

****

Life consists of many dimensions, and no one component is more or less important than the other. An exceptional life, one with meaning, is one of attempting balance and navigating a fluidity, a flow. You have permission to expand your view of life beyond work to other areas —your emotional and physical health, your relationships, your work, your spiritual well-being, and your leisure time. There is no whiteboard in the classroom of life that God has written our purpose on in which we go through life searching for. Your purpose is what you say it is.

Valorie Burton, life coach and author of <u>Successful Women Think Differently</u>, has written that your purpose is about your impact on others. Your purpose involves how someone else's life is better because they crossed your path. Your purpose is impacted by the human desire to be needed. When you are living purposefully, your job or your work may not be your purpose, but how you fulfill your responsibilities within that job is based on your identified purpose.

Creating an exceptional vision for your life can lead to increased success and joy. The qualities that can impact your success and relationships are passion and enthusiasm. When you look at some of the accomplished individuals that we encounter through literature or the media who have reached an exceptional amount of success in their lives, it is evident that they've embodied both passion and enthusiasm. The passionate and enthusiastic are empowered over those who are not. Passion and enthusiasm minimizes limitations and empowers you with the ability to influence the lives of others.

Many people spend more time planning their trip to the grocery store or vacation than they do planning their everyday life. Many do not present the essential passion and enthusiasm necessary to achieve a high level of success. A key to being truly passionate in life and awakening enthusiastically to address every task on your action plan is to create an exceptional vision for your life. Your vision should be so dynamic and powerful that there is nothing that will be an obstacle to making your vision a reality. Know that this is where your greatness lives – working toward, and seeing beyond, your current obstacles. Everyone needs an exceptional vision for their lives.

Our ultimate vision evolves from knowing that we have a special and unique purpose in life. When we pursue a vision larger than the present moment, we experience fulfillment and increased joy. So, how do you create this ultimate vision?

It's unrealistic to expect your vision to come to you overnight; a clear and well-defined vision will become clear. Determining the process that you will follow requires time and self-reflection. You need to nurture the vision and perspective, and you also need to apply intellect and planning for the application of your developed vision.

Joy will manifest itself when your vision blossoms from your dreams and aspirations. Your vision will resonate with your ideals and values and will ignite increased energy and enthusiasm to strengthen your resolve to explore the unlimited possibilities of your life.

"Action is the foundational key to all success."
—Pablo Picasso

Here are four steps to help you navigate the right paths to creating an exceptional vision for your life.

Step 1: Focus on establishing or clarifying your purpose.

If you don't do that which is necessary to clarify your purpose, you will encounter difficulty living an exceptional life that was built upon your vision. Go to an environment that inspires you and where you won't be interrupted (e.g., the park, the lake, the library). Write a paragraph or two to begin answering what you want to create for your life. Don't try to make your description perfect; you're not writing to receive an award, you're writing to create something that excites you! In addition to writing, you may want to try drawing or cutting out pictures that inspire you or that is indicative of your vision. There is no right or wrong way to describe your ultimate vision. You may want to choose a song that could become the theme song for your life.

"Some people dream of great accomplishments,
while others stay awake and do them."
—Anonymous

Step 2: Be very specific.

Your vision should provide some detail about what measurable and attainable results you are going to achieve in your life. This measurement will help you to assess where you want to be versus where you are.

Every detail counts. When you are specific, the details will propel you into making your life vision a reality. Get specific about every area of your holistic life as it relates to spirituality, emotional/physical health, relationships, work, and leisure. Being able to be very specific will ignite your passion.

Clarify your objectives (goals).

We all have our ambitions, and some are more important than others. Make a list of your five most important aspirations and circle at least one that you plan to achieve within this year. Next year, you can create another list with an additional five aspirations.

Plan your timeline and strategize.

Your strategy specifies the actions you will take in order to advance toward your goals. If your vision is to create a business, your strategy should include how to earn or save the money that you would need. Get real and direct feedback to shape and grow your business. Be realistic about the amount of time you allocate and consider all of the factors that could work for you or against you. Adhering to a timeline enables you to stay focused on your intentions.

If your vision is to lose weight, your strategy could include whether you would get a personal trainer, join a gym, use a DVD or online link, or simply workout at home. Determine how your progress will be monitored for the goal you want to accomplish. You should be realistic about your exercising and calorie intake and avoid temptations that will impede your success. Your committed discipline enables you to reach your goal.

Take your first step.

Action is required to fulfill your intentions. Although your first step may be based on faith, it is critical to take this first step and work toward proving to yourself the power of your own abilities.

> "*Motivation is what gets you started,*
> *habit is what keeps you going.*"
> —Jim Rohn

Step 3: Persevere and Stay Determined

Keep your eye on the prize and don't allow yourself to become taken off the path of accomplishing your goals. Always practice the vision that you've dreamed of so that it can become your reality. You deserve it!

Learn from setbacks.

There is a greater purpose to all occurrences in your life. Your wisdom increases when you have a higher understanding of why particular things are happening and how those things may propel you forward.

Embrace asking for help.

You may notice that unrequested help may not come at first, but when it starts flowing in, you will experience more than you imagined! Notice the people that you meet along the way.

*Do not give up!

Just having a vision does not accomplish the vision; you must work to make your dream, wish, or desire come true. You will experience speed-bumps along the way, obstacles that may slow your progress. These may intimidate you, but remember that you are on a mission to accomplish something great, and you won't let anything stop you!

*Don't repeat mistakes.

Talk show host, Oprah Winfrey, has been known to say, "When we know better, we do better." As we learn, we grow. We grow to take new actions and to avoid past actions. Learn from your mistakes and don't place yourself in situations or events which will attract the chance to repeat a known mistake.

"The most valuable thing you can make is a mistake. You can't learn anything from being perfect."
—Adam Osborne

Step 4: Be creative in your thinking and think LARGE!

The fourth step to help you create an exceptionally powerful vision for your life is to expand your thinking. If one of your major goals in life is to double your income, begin thinking in terms of finding ways to triple or quadruple your income. Take any goal that you may have, ignite your spirit, and multiply that goal. Make sure that this vision is emotionally charged, with the power to move you to action. Your vision will provide a consistent focus, continually reminding you of what it is you are committed to creating in your life, career, or business. If you feel that you have already been thinking creatively and big, think bigger! The significant goals that you set for your life that excite you have you waking every morning with an insatiable appetite to make each day a masterpiece. When was the last time you felt that way? You can recapture that feeling! If this is the first time you're exploring the possibilities, embrace and enjoy the process. You are the only one who can create the life that you deserve.

Check your emotions.

Our visions are in danger of becoming blurred when emotions are involved. Oftentimes, we can't visualize the results of something to which we're attached. When you hit a brick wall, you risk becoming stuck and can't see what's at the top of the staircase because there are other things or clutter along the way that may be obstacles in your moving forward with your vision. Your vision is blocked. This happens when your emotions create an obstacle in your progress, keeping you from anticipating what's to occur in any specific situation. By learning how to tap into your emotions and exhibit some form of emotional control, you can step away long enough to get a clearer view and see the truth of what is on the horizon that awaits you.

Create a larger version of yourself.

Oftentimes, we tend to place limitations on ourselves that define who we are or who we are not. This perspective oftentimes causes us to be satisfied with that which is less than our potential. Take the time to form a detailed, clear picture of what a larger version of your life would look like. In this version, picture yourself having already achieved your greatest goals and having fulfilled your most heart-felt desires. Imagining helps you to understand what it is that you really want.

Celebrate your accomplishments.

Reflection must be a part of your journey in creating your vision. Think about where you were five years ago and where you are now. Congratulate yourself for your achievements, both small and big. Always include rewarding yourself for your strong character, careful planning, and diligent work.

See a future of you walking through life; expanding your vision enables experiencing the full depth of what's available to you beyond what you're currently experiencing and embracing greater opportunities. Creating an exceptional vision for your life is key to be able to live with passion and enthusiasm. We oftentimes encounter obstacles in life, things that cause us to pause. Yet, when you behold an extraordinary vision for the person you aspire to be and the life that you imagine for yourself, no obstacle or failure will be able to steal your joy. You were born to add value to this world. You have an exceptional vision to create for your life!

"To create an extraordinary quality of life,
you must create a vision
that's not only obtainable, but that's sustainable."
–Anthony Robbins

Coaching Questions to Explore Creating Your Life Vision

1. *Spiritual*
-What do you want to create in your life?
-What would your life be about? What does that vision look like?
-What challenges might you be excited to overcome?

2. *Emotional/Physical*
-What do you want to give, create, be, feel, or share?
-What does the person you aspire to be look like?
-How does the person you aspire to look like interact with others?
-Where does that person spend the majority of their time?

3. *Work*
-What would get you up early in the morning and keep you up late at night?
-If you had no fear about moving forward, what would you do in your life?

4. *Relationships*

-What do you want to contribute to your own life and the lives of others?

-What's the quality of your relationships?

-What's the difference you want to make in the lives of others?

5. *Leisure*

-If you had the energy that you had as a child and your life journey had just begun, what would you be excited to tackle?

-What do you want to experience along the way?

———————————

As you journey through life, manifest your vision, act on your goals - and start to experience change. Your life's vision will continue to evolve and you'll notice the magic happen, and people may call you blessed. Clients often embrace this good fortune of the alignment of their vision and the desires of their heart. We're all capable of experiencing this blessing if we have the faith to put in the work. Get started now! You are more than your successes. You are more than your challenges. The life you were meant to live is waiting. Let us embrace life as we live it. Let's be fearless as we find joy in the journey. Waiting for you, is the life you were meant to live.

Resources

How Much Joy Can You Stand—A Creative Guide to Facing Your Fears and Making Your Dreams Come True, by Suzanne Falter-Barns. (New York: Random House, 2000).

> This humorous book gives a wealth of ways to break through the walls to creative expression and provides the inspiration that a reader needs to jump-start their life and become "un-stuck."

Joy on the Job by Doris Helge, Ph.D. (Washington: Shimoda Publishing, 2007).

> This noted author shares over 365 ways to create joy and fulfillment in the workplace.

Living a Life That Matters, by Harold S. Kushner (New York: Random House, 2001).

> This book presents the importance of making a difference in the world by affecting the life of even one person in a positive way. In doing so, we prove that we do, in fact, matter.

Successful Women Think Differently: 9-Habits to Make You Happier, Healthier, and More Resilient by Valorie Burton (Oregon: Harvest House Publishers, 2012).

> Successful women do think differently. They make decisions differently. They set goals differently and bounce back from failure differently. Burton is dedicated to help women create new thought processes that empower them to succeed in their relationships, finances, work, health, and spiritual

life. In this powerful and practical guide, Burton provides a woman with insight into who she really is and gives her the tools, knowledge, and understanding to succeed.

The Secret by Rhonda Byrne (New York: Simon & Schuster, 2006).

Fragments of a great secret have been found in the oral traditions, in literature, in religions, and in philosophies throughout the centuries. In this book, you'll learn how to use *The Secret* in every aspect of your life – money, health, relationships, happiness, and every interaction you have in the world. You'll begin to understand the hidden, untapped power that's within you, and this revelation can bring joy to every aspect of your life. *The Secret* contains wisdom from modern-day teachers – men and women who have used it to achieve health, wealth, and happiness.

Online Resource

http://www.entrepreneur.com/author/matt-mayberry

Matt Mayberry Enterprises provides performance strategies and specializes in helping individuals and organizations escape mediocrity and claim their greatness.

In this book, **How Much Joy Is In Your Journey? A Creative Guide to Your Fearless Vision**, Dr. Ja'net Bishop inspires you to embark on the journey to create a vision for your life and experience more joy toward achieving your goals – and realizing your dreams!

Her company:

>HAVE JOY, LLC
>Certified Personal & Executive Coach;
>author; and inspirational speaker

Her virtual services:

>Individual and Group Coaching Programs
>Teleseminar/Webinar, and eCourse Programs

Her additional services:

>Keynotes, Seminars, and Workshops

Her contact information:

Phone:	(762)-233-1118
Email:	janet@HaveJoyLLC.com
Email:	dr.janet.bishop@gmail.com
Website:	www.HaveJoyLLC.com
FACEBOOK-Business	Have Joy, LLC
FACEBOOK-Public	Ja'net Bishop
TWITTER	@drjanetbishop
LinkedIn	Dr. Ja'net Bishop

ABOUT THE AUTHOR

Dr. Ja'net Bishop is the CEO and Founder of **Have Joy, LLC**. She's a *Certified Personal & Executive Coach* providing self-development and empowerment coaching to support her client's strengths and assist them in using those strengths to move forward with their goals, *"live on purpose"*, and not compromise their quality of life. She has presented keynotes, seminars, and workshops in various venues (college, local, state, and national conferences). Her topics have addressed work/life balance, school culture/climate, collaborations, and at-risk youth issues.

Ja'net, is a native of New York and a former military officer. Her 20+ years in the Education and Human Service fields, reflects her experience working in non-profits. She has served as a certified school counselor (middle, high, and alternative settings), and as a high school principal in both a traditional and alternative setting.
A former adjunct professor for Cambridge College, she has taught and advised aspiring school counselors enrolled in the Counselor Education graduate program. Ja'net has also served as a consultant to the local Juvenile Court.

Ja'net is Board Director-Region 3 on the National Alternative Education Association (NAEA) board. She is also the former President-Elect of the Georgia Association of Alternative Education (GAAE). Additionally, Ja'net is the Vice-Commander and Treasurer of the Military Order of World Wars-Augusta, Georgia Chapter, and serves on the Eagle Scout Review Board-Columbia County, Georgia, both of which support youth leadership programs.

An alumni of *Leadership Augusta* through the Chamber of Commerce, Ja'net advocates for youth leadership initiatives and has judged various academic pageants. She believes that everyone has the potential to develop character, leadership, and to live life on purpose! She and her husband William (also a school administrator) are the proud parents of two sons, William II and Matthew, whom she considers to be the true blessed accomplishments of her life!

ACKNOWLEDGMENTS

Throughout my life, I have been blessed to have shared a connection with so many people who have encouraged me both personally and professionally. The love and wisdom I've received have been channeled into this book. The list could fill volumes and because I am afraid of inadvertently forgetting someone, let me state first and foremost that I am deeply grateful for each and every one of you for your prayers and support.

Every writer needs that special person to silence the inner-critic that tugs away at you as you write and fall into "analysis paralysis." Tierica Berry has been that person as my Author Coach. She provided seasoned skill, guidance and encouragement.

Cudos to my virtual assistant, Nitara Deratany, who created my Social Media presence, as I am not a "Techie" and her skill-set has been priceless.

Thanks to my friend, Margaret Adams, whose spiritual insight and faith has been empowering.

A special thank you to Roslyn Ferrell, my sister-friend since I was five years old. She always knew the perfect thing to say – with wit and humor that only we understood!

My heartfelt gratitude, thanks, and appreciation to my husband, William, as we supported each other through our life's journey. We've navigated through raising a family, pursuing dreams, accomplishing goals, and the creation of this book. He is my friend and my love. Together, we embrace, with a full heart, the blessed joy in our lives - our sons William II and Matthew.

I thank God for all of the blessings in my journey through life.
Live life on purpose – with Joy!